CW00540639

# HCG COOKBOOK

**40+Tart, Ice-Cream, and Pie recipes for a healthy and balanced HCG diet**

# TABLE OF CONTENTS

advice is necessary, legal or professional, a practiced individual in the profession should be ordered.

- From a Declaration of Principles which was accepted and approved equally by a Committee of the American Bar Association and a Committee of Publishers and Associations.

Introduction

HCG recipes for personal enjoyment but also for family enjoyment. You will love them for sure for how easy it is to prepare them.

# *BREAKFAST RECIPES*

## PUMPKIN CUPCAKES

Serves: **4**

Prep Time: **10** Minutes

Cook Time: **30** Minutes

Total Time: **40** Minutes

### INGREDIENTS

- 1 cup pumpkin puree
- 1 tsp cinnamon
- ½ tsp mixed spice
- 1 tsp ginger
- ¼ lb. butter
- 1 cups brown sugar
- 2 eggs
- 2 cups flour
- 3 tsp baking powder

### DIRECTIONS

1. Boil the pumpkin and then puree in a food processor
2. Cream butter and sugar, add the eggs and beat well, stir in pureed pumpkin and dry ingredients
3. Combine all ingredients and spoon mixture into a muffin tin

4. Bake at 300 F for 20 minutes, remove and serve

# BUCKWHEAT PANCAKES

Serves:          **2**

Prep Time:    **10**   Minutes

Cook Time:    **10**   Minutes

Total Time:   **20**   Minutes

## INGREDIENTS

- 1 cup buckwheat mix
- 1 egg
- 1 cup milk
- 1 tablespoon butter

## DIRECTIONS

1. In a bow mix all ingredients, add olive oil and pour batter
2. Cook for 1-2 minutes per side
3. Remove and serve

# CARROT CAKE

Serves: **4**

Prep Time: **10** Minutes

Cook Time: **40** Minutes

Total Time: **50** Minutes

## INGREDIENTS

- 1 cup whole meal self raising flour
- 1 cup brown sugar
- 1 cup self raising flour
- 1 tsp salt
- 1 tsp cinnamon
- 1 tsp ginger
- 1 cup olive oil
- 2 cups carrots
- 3 eggs
- ½ tsp allspice

## DIRECTIONS

1. Preheat oven to 275 F and place all ingredients in a bowl except eggs
2. In another bowl mix eggs and add to the mixture
3. Pour into cake in
4. For carrot cake pour batter into cupcake molds

5. Bake for 40 minutes
6. Remove and serve

# RUSSIAN FUDGE

Serves:         *2*
Prep Time:   *10*   Minutes

Cook Time:   *30*   Minutes

Total Time:  *40*   Minutes

## INGREDIENTS

- ½ butter
- 1 can condensed milk
- ¾ cup milk
- 2 tablespoons golden syrup
- 3 cups sugar
- 1 tablespoon vanilla essence

## DIRECTIONS

1. In a pot place all the ingredients except vanilla essence and bring to boil
2. Boil for 15-20 minutes and in another bowl drop some fudge mixture
3. Add vanilla essence and beat with a mixer for 5-6 minutes
4. Pour into greased tin and place in fridge
5. Cut into pieces and serve

# GINGER BEER

Serves:        *2*
Prep Time:    *10*   Minutes

Cook Time:   *20*   Minutes

Total Time:   *30*   Minutes

## INGREDIENTS

- 1-inch ginger
- 4 tablespoons brown sugar
- 1 tsp citric acid
- 1 L soda water
- fresh mint

## DIRECTIONS

1. Grate ginger and mix with the rest of ingredients and let them sit for 10-12 minutes
2. Serve when ready

# CINNAMON SCONES

Serves: **4**

Prep Time: **10** Minutes

Cook Time: **30** Minutes

Total Time: **40** Minutes

## INGREDIENTS

- 2 cups self raising flour
- 2 tablespoons butter
- 2/3 cups milk

### FILLING

- 1/3 cup butter
- ¾ cup brown sugar
- 1 tsp cinnamon

## DIRECTIONS

1. Preheat oven to 350 F
2. In a blender add butter, flour and blend until smooth
3. Add milk and blend or another 1-2 minutes
4. Remove mixture onto floured surface
5. In the blender put all ingredients for the filling and blend until smooth
6. Spread the filling into the dough

Serves: **4**

Prep Time: **10** Minutes

Cook Time: **30** Minutes

Total Time: **40** Minutes

### INGREDIENTS

- 1 leek
- 1 clove garlic
- sat
- citric acid
- 1 tsp turmeric
- 1 tsp cumin
- 1 tsp coriander powder
- ½ cup roasted sunflower seeds
- 1 tablespoon rice flour
- 1 tsp arrowroot
- 1 cup broccoli
- 2 tablespoons butter
- 1 cup milk
- macaroni pasta

## DIRECTIONS

1.  Cook pasta, add leek and sauté with butter, citric acid and pepper
2.  Add butter, cumin, coriander powder, turmeric, sunflower seeds
3.  Add arrowroot and rice flour and cook for 2-3 minutes
4.  Add broccoli, pasta and stir
5.  Cook for 20 minutes at 350 F, remove and serve

# SPRING ROLLS

Serves:       **4**
Prep Time:   **10**  Minutes

Cook Time:  **20**  Minutes

Total Time:  **30**  Minutes

## INGREDIENTS

- rice noodles
- onion
- cucumber
- carrot
- Coriander
- zucchini
- carrot
- Thai mint
- Chives
- Roasted sunflower seeds
- ginger
- rice paper
- tofu

## DIRECTIONS

1. In a bowl place the noodles and boil, cover with a lid

2. When they are cool set aside, soak a couple of rice papers in warm water and place the rice paper on a towel

3. Place the noodles and the rest of rest of ingredients on a rice paper and fold

4. Serve when ready

Serves:          **4**
Prep Time:    **10**   Minutes

Cook Time:    **30**   Minutes

Total Time:   **40**   Minutes

## INGREDIENTS

- ¼ lb. butter
- ½ cup sugar
- 1 cup plain flour
- ½ whole meal flour
- 1 tsp baking powder
- 1 tsp ginger

## DIRECTIONS

1. In a food processor add butter and soon and blend until smooth
2. Add the rest of ingredients and blend
3. Remove from blender and bake for 20 minutes at 350 F
4. Cut into cookie shape and serve

Serves: **2**

Prep Time: **10** Minutes

Cook Time: **10** Minutes

Total Time: **20** Minutes

## INGREDIENTS

- 1 cup corn flour
- 1 egg
- 1 cup milk
- 1 tablespoon butter
- 2 tablespoons honey
- ½ cup rice flour
- 1 tsp baking powder
- ½ tsp salt

## DIRECTIONS

1. Let sit for 8-10 minutes
2. Place in the waffle iron and cook
3. Remove and serve

# CHEESE CAKE

Serves:          *4*

Prep Time:    *10*   Minutes

Cook Time:    *30*   Minutes

Total Time:    *40*   Minutes

## INGREDIENTS

- ½ lb. gingernut biscuits
- ½ lb. blueberries
- 1 tsp vanilla extract
- 1 tsp acid
- ¼ lb. butter
- ¼ lb. caster sugar
- 2 tablespoons arrowroot
- ¼ lb. full-fat Philadelphia
- 2 eggs

## DIRECTIONS

1. Preheat oven to 350 F
2. In a bowl mix butter and biscuits and press into the base of the tin
3. Bake for 10-12 minutes
4. In a saucepan cook blueberry with sugar and milk for 10-12 minutes

5. Take off heat add citric acid and vanilla
6. Bake for 40 minutes remove and let it chill

# BASIC WAFFLES

Serves: **2**
Prep Time: **10** Minutes

Cook Time: **10** Minutes

Total Time: **20** Minutes

## INGREDIENTS

- 2 eggs
- 1 tablespoon sugar
- 1 tablespoon baking powder
- 1 cup flour
- 1/8 cup milk
- ½ tsp vanilla essence

## DIRECTIONS

1. In a food processor add all the ingredients and blend until smooth
2. Heat the waffle iron pour in the batter
3. Cook until golden
4. Serve with maple syrup

# CARAMEL POPCORN

Serves:          **4**

Prep Time:    **10**   Minutes

Cook Time:    **20**   Minutes

Total Time:    **30**   Minutes

## INGREDIENTS

- 1 tablespoon olive oil
- 4 tablespoons popcorn kernels

CARAMEL SAUCE

- 1 tablespoon butter
- 1 tablespoon brown sugar
- 1 tablespoon golden syrup

## DIRECTIONS

1. In a saucepan pour olive oil and popcorn kernels over medium heat and cover
2. Shake the saucepan to distribute evenly
3. In another saucepan melt the caramel sauce ingredients
4. Remove from heat and pour over your popcorn

# ONION PANCAKES

Serves:          *4*
Prep Time:   *10*   Minutes

Cook Time:   *10*   Minutes

Total Time:   *20*   Minutes

## INGREDIENTS

- ½ tsp salt
- 1 cup plain flour
- 1 tsp olive oil
- 1 onion
- ½ cup hot water
- 1 tablespoon cold water

## DIRECTIONS

1. In a bowl mix all ingredients
2. Pour mixture into a pan and cook for 1-2 minutes per side
3. Remove and serve

# TOASTED MUESLI

Serves:        **4**
Prep Time:    **10**   Minutes

Cook Time:    **60**   Minutes

Total Time:   **70**   Minutes

## INGREDIENTS

- 2 cups oats
- 1 cup oat mix
- ½ cup sunflower seeds
- ½ cup sunflower oil

## DIRECTIONS

1. **In a bowl mix all ingredients**
2. **Bake for 60 minutes at 275 F**
3. **Garnish with blueberries and serve**

# GINGERBREAD BISCUITS

Serves:          **4**

Prep Time:   **10**   Minutes

Cook Time:   **30**   Minutes

Total Time:   **40**   Minutes

## INGREDIENTS

- 2 oz. butter
- 1 cup self raising flour
- ½ tsp salt
- 3 tablespoons ginger
- ½ cup milk
- 1 egg beaten
- 1 tablespoon vanilla extract
- ½ cup golden syrup
- ½ cup maple syrup
- ½ cup honey

## DIRECTIONS

1. Preheat oven to 300 F
2. In a pan melt honey, butter, syrup and set aside
3. White syrup mixture is cooling, grate the ginger and add to the syrup mixture
4. Add flour, salt, milk, egg and vanilla extract

5. Form small cookies and bake for 15-18 minutes at 300 F
6. Remove and serve

# VANILLA CHIA PUDDING

Serves:           **4**

Prep Time:   **10**   Minutes

Cook Time:   **10**   Minutes

Total Time:   **20**   Minutes

## INGREDIENTS

- 2 cups hemp milk
- 2 packets stevia
- ½ tsp cinnamon
- ½ cup chia seeds
- 1 tablespoon vanilla extract

## DIRECTIONS

1. In a bowl whisk all ingredients together
2. Let it chill overnight and serve

# APPLE PANCAKES

Serves: **4**

Prep Time: **10** Minutes

Cook Time: **20** Minutes

Total Time: **30** Minutes

## INGREDIENTS

- 1 cup whole wheat flour
- ¼ tsp baking soda
- ¼ tsp baking powder
- 1 cup apples
- 2 eggs
- 1 cup milk

## DIRECTIONS

1. In a bowl combine all ingredients together and mix well
2. In a skillet heat olive oil
3. Pour ¼ of the batter and cook each pancake for 1-2 minutes per side
4. When ready remove from heat and serve

# APRICOTS PANCAKES

Serves:          **4**

Prep Time:    **10**   Minutes

Cook Time:   **30**   Minutes

Total Time:   **40**   Minutes

## INGREDIENTS

- 1 cup whole wheat flour
- ¼ tsp baking soda
- ¼ tsp baking powder
- 1 cup apricots
- 2 eggs
- 1 cup milk

## DIRECTIONS

1. In a bowl combine all ingredients together and mix well
2. In a skillet heat olive oil
3. Pour ¼ of the batter and cook each pancake for 1-2 minutes per side
4. When ready remove from heat and serve

# ACEROLA PANCAKES

Serves:          *4*

Prep Time:    *10*   Minutes

Cook Time:   *20*   Minutes

Total Time:   *30*   Minutes

## INGREDIENTS

- 1 cup whole wheat flour
- ¼ tsp baking soda
- ¼ tsp baking powder
- 1 cup acerola
- 2 eggs
- 1 cup milk

## DIRECTIONS

1. In a bowl combine all ingredients together and mix well
2. In a skillet heat olive oil
3. Pour ¼ of the batter and cook each pancake for 1-2 minutes per side
4. When ready remove from heat and serve

# JAVA-PLUM MUFFINS

Serves:        *8-12*
Prep Time:    *10*   Minutes

Cook Time:   *20*   Minutes

Total Time:    *30*   Minutes

## INGREDIENTS

- 2 eggs
- 1 tablespoon olive oil
- 1 cup milk
- 2 cups whole wheat flour
- 1 tsp baking soda
- ¼ tsp baking soda
- 1 tsp cinnamon
- 1 cup java-plum

## DIRECTIONS

1. In a bowl combine all dry ingredients
2. In another bowl combine all dry ingredients
3. Combine wet and dry ingredients together
4. Pour mixture into 8-12 prepared muffin cups, fill 2/3 of the cups
5. Bake for 18-20 minutes at 375 F
6. When ready remove from the oven and serve

# KIWI MUFFINS

Serves:        **8-12**

Prep Time:     **10**    Minutes

Cook Time:     **20**    Minutes

Total Time:    **30**    Minutes

## INGREDIENTS

- 2 eggs
- 1 tablespoon olive oil
- 1 cup milk
- 2 cups whole wheat flour
- 1 tsp baking soda
- ¼ tsp baking soda
- 1 tsp cinnamon
- 1 cup kiwi

## DIRECTIONS

1. In a bowl combine all dry ingredients
2. In another bowl combine all dry ingredients
3. Combine wet and dry ingredients together
4. Pour mixture into 8-12 prepared muffin cups, fill 2/3 of the cups
5. Bake for 18-20 minutes at 375 F
6. When ready remove from the oven and serve

# CHOCOLATE MUFFINS

Serves:          *8-12*
Prep Time:    *10*   Minutes

Cook Time:   *20*   Minutes

Total Time:   *30*   Minutes

## INGREDIENTS

- 2 eggs
- 1 tablespoon olive oil
- 1 cup milk
- 2 cups whole wheat flour
- 1 tsp baking soda
- ¼ tsp baking soda
- 1 tsp cinnamon
- 1 cup chocolate chips

## DIRECTIONS

1. In a bowl combine all dry ingredients
2. In another bowl combine all dry ingredients
3. Combine wet and dry ingredients together
4. Pour mixture into 8-12 prepared muffin cups, fill 2/3 of the cups
5. Bake for 18-20 minutes at 375 F
6. When ready remove from the oven and serve

# MANGO MUFFINS

Serves:        *8-12*
Prep Time:     *10*   Minutes

Cook Time:     *20*   Minutes

Total Time:    *30*   Minutes

## INGREDIENTS

- 2 eggs
- 1 tablespoon olive oil
- 1 cup milk
- 2 cups whole wheat flour
- 1 tsp baking soda
- ¼ tsp baking soda
- 1 tsp cinnamon
- 1 cup mango

## DIRECTIONS

1. In a bowl combine all dry ingredients
2. In another bowl combine all dry ingredients
3. Combine wet and dry ingredients together
4. Pour mixture into 8-12 prepared muffin cups, fill 2/3 of the cups
5. Bake for 18-20 minutes at 375 F
6. When ready remove from the oven and serve

# BOK CHOY OMELETTE

Serves:           *1*
Prep Time:     5     Minutes

Cook Time:   *10*   Minutes

Total Time:   *15*   Minutes

## INGREDIENTS

- 2 eggs
- ¼ tsp salt
- ¼ tsp black pepper
- 1 tablespoon olive oil
- ¼ cup cheese
- ¼ tsp basil
- 1 cup bok choy

## DIRECTIONS

1. In a bowl combine all ingredients together and mix well
2. In a skillet heat olive oil and pour the egg mixture
3. Cook for 1-2 minutes per side
4. When ready remove omelette from the skillet and serve

# BRUSSEL SPROUTS OMELETTE

Serves:        *1*
Prep Time:    5    Minutes

Cook Time:   *10*   Minutes

Total Time:   *15*   Minutes

## INGREDIENTS

- 2 eggs
- ¼ tsp salt
- ¼ tsp black pepper
- 1 tablespoon olive oil
- ¼ cup cheese
- ¼ tsp basil
- 1 cup Brussel sprouts

## DIRECTIONS

1. In a bowl combine all ingredients together and mix well
2. In a skillet heat olive oil and pour the egg mixture
3. Cook for 1-2 minutes per side
4. When ready remove omelette from the skillet and serve

# CARROT OMELETTE

Serves:         *1*
Prep Time:    5   Minutes

Cook Time:   *10*   Minutes

Total Time:  *15*   Minutes

## INGREDIENTS

- 2 eggs
- ¼ tsp salt
- ¼ tsp black pepper
- 1 tablespoon olive oil
- ¼ cup cheese
- ¼ tsp basil
- 1 cup carrot

## DIRECTIONS

1. In a bowl combine all ingredients together and mix well
2. In a skillet heat olive oil and pour the egg mixture
3. Cook for 1-2 minutes per side
4. When ready remove omelette from the skillet and serve

# CORN OMELETTE

Serves:        *1*
Prep Time:    *5*    Minutes

Cook Time:   *10*   Minutes

Total Time:   *15*   Minutes

## INGREDIENTS

- 2 eggs
- ¼ tsp salt
- ¼ tsp black pepper
- 1 tablespoon olive oil
- ¼ cup cheese
- ¼ tsp basil
- 1 cup corn

## DIRECTIONS

1. In a bowl combine all ingredients together and mix well
2. In a skillet heat olive oil and pour the egg mixture
3. Cook for 1-2 minutes per side
4. When ready remove omelette from the skillet and serve

# EGGPLANT OMELETTE

Serves:          *1*
Prep Time:    *5*    Minutes

Cook Time:   *10*   Minutes

Total Time:  *15*   Minutes

## INGREDIENTS

- 2 eggs
- ¼ tsp salt
- ¼ tsp black pepper
- 1 tablespoon olive oil
- ¼ cup cheese
- ¼ tsp basil
- 1 cup eggplant

## DIRECTIONS

1. In a bowl combine all ingredients together and mix well
2. In a skillet heat olive oil and pour the egg mixture
3. Cook for 1-2 minutes per side
4. When ready remove omelette from the skillet and serve

## APPLE TART

Serves:        *6-8*

Prep Time:   **25**   Minutes

Cook Time:   **25**   Minutes

Total Time:  **50**   Minutes

### INGREDIENTS

- pastry sheets

### FILLING

- 1 tsp lemon juice
- 3 oz. brown sugar
- 1 lb. apples
- 150 ml double cream
- 2 eggs

### DIRECTIONS

1. Preheat oven to 400 F, unfold pastry sheets and place them on a baking sheet
2. Toss together all ingredients together and mix well
3. Spread mixture in a single layer on the pastry sheets
4. Before baking decorate with your desired fruits
5. Bake at 400 F for 22-25 minutes or until golden brown

6.  When ready remove from the oven and serve

# CHOCHOLATE TART

Serves: **6-8**

Prep Time: **25** Minutes

Cook Time: **25** Minutes

Total Time: **50** Minutes

## INGREDIENTS

- pastry sheets
- 1 tsp vanilla extract
- ½ lb. caramel
- ½ lb. black chocolate
- 4-5 tablespoons butter
- 3 eggs
- ¼ lb. brown sugar

## DIRECTIONS

1. Preheat oven to 400 F, unfold pastry sheets and place them on a baking sheet
2. Toss together all ingredients together and mix well
3. Spread mixture in a single layer on the pastry sheets
4. Before baking decorate with your desired fruits
5. Bake at 400 F for 22-25 minutes or until golden brown
6. When ready remove from the oven and serve

# *PIE RECIPES*

## PEACH PECAN PIE

Serves: **8-12**

Prep Time: **15** Minutes

Cook Time: **35** Minutes

Total Time: **50** Minutes

### INGREDIENTS

- 4-5 cups peaches
- 1 tablespoon preserves
- 1 cup sugar
- 4 small egg yolks
- ¼ cup flour
- 1 tsp vanilla extract

### DIRECTIONS

1. Line a pie plate or pie form with pastry and cover the edges of the plate depending on your preference
2. In a bowl combine all pie ingredients together and mix well
3. Pour the mixture over the pastry
4. Bake at 400-425 F for 25-30 minutes or until golden brown
5. When ready remove from the oven and let it rest for 15 minutes

# OREO PIE

Serves: **8-12**

Prep Time: **15** Minutes

Cook Time: **35** Minutes

Total Time: **50** Minutes

## INGREDIENTS

- pastry sheets
- 6-8 oz. chocolate crumb piecrust
- 1 cup half-and-half
- 1 package instant pudding mix
- 10-12 Oreo cookies
- 10 oz. whipped topping

## DIRECTIONS

1. Line a pie plate or pie form with pastry and cover the edges of the plate depending on your preference
2. In a bowl combine all pie ingredients together and mix well
3. Pour the mixture over the pastry
4. Bake at 400-425 F for 25-30 minutes or until golden brown
5. When ready remove from the oven and let it rest for 15 minutes

# GRAPEFRUIT PIE

Serves:         *8-12*

Prep Time:    *15*    Minutes

Cook Time:    *35*    Minutes

Total Time:    *50*    Minutes

## INGREDIENTS

- pastry sheets
- 2 cups grapefruit
- 1 cup brown sugar
- ¼ cup flour
- 5-6 egg yolks
- 5 oz. butter

## DIRECTIONS

1. Line a pie plate or pie form with pastry and cover the edges of the plate depending on your preference
2. In a bowl combine all pie ingredients together and mix well
3. Pour the mixture over the pastry
4. Bake at 400-425 F for 25-30 minutes or until golden brown
5. When ready remove from the oven and let it rest for 15 minutes

# BUTTERFINGER PIE

Serves:        *8-12*

Prep Time:    *15*    Minutes

Cook Time:    *35*    Minutes

Total Time:    *50*    Minutes

## INGREDIENTS

- pastry sheets
- 1 package cream cheese
- 1 tsp vanilla extract
- ¼ cup peanut butter
- 1 cup powdered sugar (to decorate)
- 2 cups Butterfinger candy bars
- 8 oz whipped topping

## DIRECTIONS

1. Line a pie plate or pie form with pastry and cover the edges of the plate depending on your preference
2. In a bowl combine all pie ingredients together and mix well
3. Pour the mixture over the pastry
4. Bake at 400-425 F for 25-30 minutes or until golden brown
5. When ready remove from the oven and let it rest for 15 minutes

## CREAMSICLE SMOOTHIE

Serves:         *1*
Prep Time:    *5*    Minutes

Cook Time:   *5*    Minutes

Total Time:   *10*   Minutes

### INGREDIENTS

- 2 cups mango
- 1 carrot
- 1 tablespoon apple cider vinegar
- 1 tsp lemon juice
- 1 cup coconut milk
- 1 tsp honey

### DIRECTIONS

1. In a blender place all ingredients and blend until smooth
2. Pour smoothie in a glass and serve

# BUTTERMILK SMOOTHIE

Serves:        *1*

Prep Time:   5   Minutes

Cook Time:   5   Minutes

Total Time:  *10*  Minutes

## INGREDIENTS

- 1 cup strawberries
- 1 cup buttermilk
- 1 cup ice
- 1 tsp honey
- 1 tsp agave syrup

## DIRECTIONS

1. In a blender place all ingredients and blend until smooth
2. Pour smoothie in a glass and serve

# PARSLEY & PINEAPPLE SMOOTHIE

Serves:          *1*

Prep Time:    *5*    Minutes

Cook Time:   *5*    Minutes

Total Time:   *10*   Minutes

## INGREDIENTS

- 1 banana
- 1 cup pineapple
- ¼ cup parsley
- 1 tsp chia seeds
- 1 cup ice

## DIRECTIONS

1. In a blender place all ingredients and blend until smooth
2. Pour smoothie in a glass and serve

# POMEGRANATE SMOOTHIE

Serves:        *1*

Prep Time:    5   Minutes

Cook Time:   5   Minutes

Total Time:  *10*   Minutes

## INGREDIENTS

- 1 cup pomegranate juice
- ¼ cup vanilla yogurt
- 3 cooked beets
- ¼ cup grapefruit juice
- 1 tablespoon honey
- 1 cup ice

## DIRECTIONS

1. In a blender place all ingredients and blend until smooth
2. Pour smoothie in a glass and serve

# CASHEW SMOOTHIE

Serves:        *1*
Prep Time:     *5*   Minutes

Cook Time:     *5*   Minutes

Total Time:   *10*   Minutes

## INGREDIENTS

- 1 cup cashew milk
- 1 cup vanilla yogurt
- 1 banana
- 1 cup pumpkin puree
- 1 cup ice

## DIRECTIONS

1. In a blender place all ingredients and blend until smooth
2. Pour smoothie in a glass and serve

## PISTACHIOS ICE-CREAM

Serves:          **6-8**

Prep Time:    **15**    Minutes

Cook Time:    **15**    Minutes

Total Time:    **30**    Minutes

### INGREDIENTS

- 4 egg yolks
- 1 cup heavy cream
- 1 cup milk
- 1 cup sugar
- 1 vanilla bean
- 1 tsp almond extract
- 1 cup cherries
- ½ cup pistachios

### DIRECTIONS

1. In a saucepan whisk together all ingredients
2. Mix until bubbly
3. Strain into a bowl and cool
4. Whisk in favorite fruits and mix well
5. Cover and refrigerate for 2-3 hours

6. Pour mixture in the ice-cream maker and follow manufacturer instructions
7. Serve when ready

# VANILLA ICE-CREAM

Serves:       *6-8*

Prep Time:    *15*   Minutes
Cook Time:    *15*   Minutes
Total Time:   *30*   Minutes

## INGREDIENTS

- 1 cup milk
- 1 tablespoon cornstarch
- 1 oz. cream cheese
- 1 cup heavy cream
- 1 cup brown sugar
- 1 tablespoon corn syrup
- 1 vanilla bean

## DIRECTIONS

1. In a saucepan whisk together all ingredients
2. Mix until bubbly
3. Strain into a bowl and cool
4. Whisk in favorite fruits and mix well
5. Cover and refrigerate for 2-3 hours
6. Pour mixture in the ice-cream maker and follow manufacturer instructions
7. Serve when ready

*THANK YOU FOR READING THIS BOOK!*

CPSIA information can be obtained
at www.ICGtesting.com
Printed in the USA
BVHW031013150321
602551BV00004B/283

9 781664 057265